D1126184

BY THOMAS K. ADAMSON

THE NEW ENGLAND
PATRIOTS
STORY

TORQUE

BELLWETHER MEDIA · MINNEAPOLIS, MN

Are you ready to take it to the extreme? Torque books thrust you into the action-packed world of sports, vehicles, mystery, and adventure. These books may include dirt, smoke, fire, and chilling tales. **WARNING**: read at your own risk.

This edition first published in 2017 by Bellwether Media, Inc.

No part of this publication may be reproduced in whole or in part without written permission of the publisher. For information regarding permission, write to Bellwether Media, Inc., Attention: Permissions Department, 5357 Penn Avenue South, Minneapolis, MN 55419.

Library of Congress Cataloging-in-Publication Data

Names: Adamson, Thomas K., 1970-
Title: The New England Patriots Story / by Thomas K. Adamson.
Description: Minneapolis, MN : Bellwether Media, Inc., 2017. | Series:
   Torque: NFL Teams | Includes bibliographical references and index. |
   Audience: Ages: 7-12. | Audience: Grades: 3-7.
Identifiers: LCCN 2016000136 | ISBN 9781626173736 (hardcover : alk. paper)
Subjects: LCSH: New England Patriots (Football team)–History–Juvenile
   literature.
Classification: LCC GV956.N36 A33 2017 | DDC 796.332/640974461–dc23
LC record available at http://lccn.loc.gov/2016000136

Printed in the United States of America, North Mankato, MN.

TABLE OF CONTENTS

On February 1, 2015, the **New England** Patriots face the Seattle Seahawks in **Super Bowl** 49. The Patriots are behind 14 to 24 going into the fourth quarter.

Tom Brady

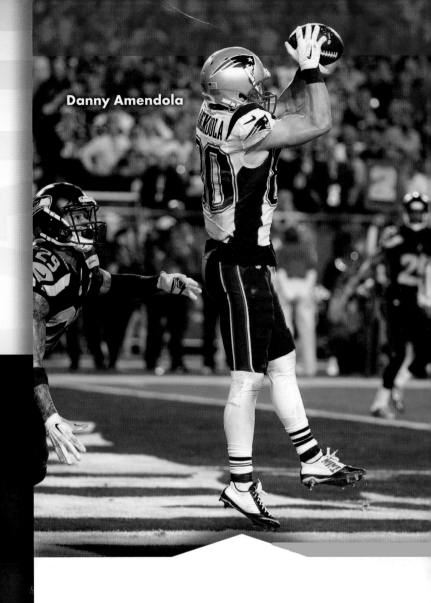

Danny Amendola

Quarterback Tom Brady throws a touchdown pass to **wide receiver** Danny Amendola. The Patriots are now only 3 points behind.

Malcolm Butler

Late in the game, Brady throws another touchdown. The Patriots take the lead! The Seahawks storm down the field with the ball. They only have 26 seconds left to try to win the game.

Seattle's quarterback sends a pass into the end zone. Patriots' **cornerback** Malcolm Butler snatches the ball. **Interception**! The clock runs out and the Patriots win!

SCORING TERMS

END ZONE

the area at each end of a football field; a team scores by entering the opponent's end zone with the football.

EXTRA POINT

a score that occurs when a kicker kicks the ball between the opponent's goal posts after a touchdown is scored; 1 point.

FIELD GOAL

a score that occurs when a kicker kicks the ball between the opponent's goal posts; 3 points.

SAFETY

a score that occurs when a player on offense is tackled behind his own goal line; 2 points for defense.

TOUCHDOWN

a score that occurs when a team crosses into its opponent's end zone with the football; 6 points.

TWO-POINT CONVERSION

a score that occurs when a team crosses into its opponent's end zone with the football after scoring a touchdown; 2 points.

The New England Patriots won their first Super Bowl in 2002. No one realized it was the start of a football **dynasty**. But success had not been easy.

The Patriots struggled to win for most of their history. In 1990, the team only won one game. But after 2000, they started to win many championships.

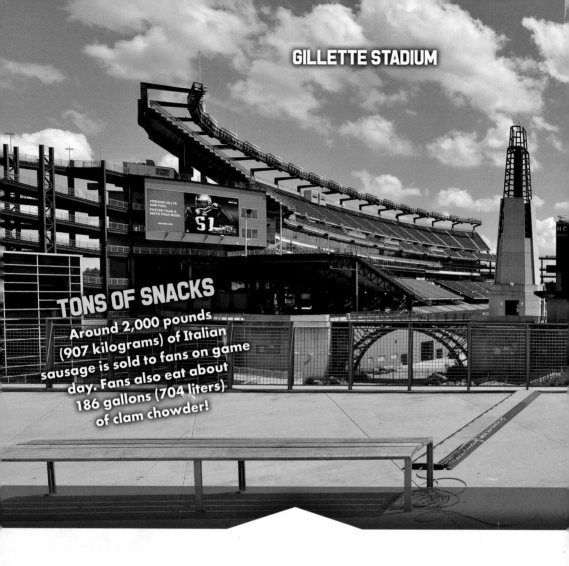

GILLETTE STADIUM

TONS OF SNACKS

Around 2,000 pounds (907 kilograms) of Italian sausage is sold to fans on game day. Fans also eat about 186 gallons (704 liters) of clam chowder!

The Patriots play their home games in Foxborough, Massachusetts, near Boston. For 30 years, they played at Foxboro Stadium. Gillette Stadium replaced it in 2002.

Gillette has many improvements over Foxboro. It offers comfortable seating, more parking, and better food for fans.

FOXBOROUGH, MASSACHUSETTS

The Patriots play in the East **Division** of the American Football **Conference** (AFC). Their main **rival** is the New York Jets.

In 1997, New England's head coach Bill Parcells switched sides. He left the Patriots to coach the Jets!

NFL DIVISIONS

 AFC

AFC NORTH

BALTIMORE **RAVENS**	CINCINNATI **BENGALS**
CLEVELAND **BROWNS**	PITTSBURGH **STEELERS**

AFC EAST

BUFFALO **BILLS**	MIAMI **DOLPHINS**
NEW ENGLAND **PATRIOTS**	NEW YORK **JETS**

AFC SOUTH

HOUSTON **TEXANS**	INDIANAPOLIS **COLTS**
JACKSONVILLE **JAGUARS**	TENNESSEE **TITANS**

AFC WEST

DENVER **BRONCOS**	KANSAS CITY **CHIEFS**
OAKLAND **RAIDERS**	SAN DIEGO **CHARGERS**

MORE FOR THE RIVALRY

Bill Belichick coached the Jets for a day before becoming the Patriots' head coach!

NFC

NFC NORTH

 CHICAGO **BEARS**

 DETROIT **LIONS**

 GREEN BAY **PACKERS**

 MINNESOTA **VIKINGS**

NFC EAST

 DALLAS **COWBOYS**

 NEW YORK **GIANTS**

 PHILADELPHIA **EAGLES**

 WASHINGTON **REDSKINS**

NFC SOUTH

 ATLANTA **FALCONS**

 CAROLINA **PANTHERS**

NEW ORLEANS **SAINTS**

TAMPA BAY **BUCCANEERS**

NFC WEST

 ARIZONA **CARDINALS**

LOS ANGELES **RAMS**

 SAN FRANCISCO **49ERS**

 SEATTLE **SEAHAWKS**

The Boston Patriots were one of the original American Football League (AFL) teams in 1960. They joined the National Football League (NFL) in 1970.

Soon after, the team was renamed the New England Patriots. The team had many rough seasons in the 1980s and 1990s.

1965 season

In 2000, the Patriots gained one of the best quarterback-head coach combinations in the league. They **drafted** Tom Brady and hired Bill Belichick.

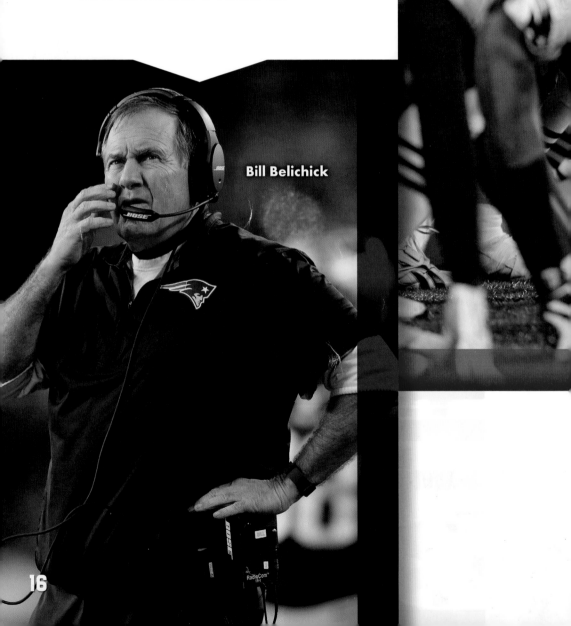

Bill Belichick

BEST REGULAR SEASON

In 2007, the Patriots completed the best regular season in NFL history. They went 16-0!

The team stunned everyone when they won Super Bowl 36 in 2002. They won two more Super Bowls in the next three years!

PATRIOTS TIMELINE

1960
First played in the AFL as the Boston Patriots

1971
Changed team name to New England Patriots

1993
Revealed new logo and changed main color from red to blue

2000
Hired head coach Bill Belichick

1971
First played in Foxboro Stadium (then called Schaefer Stadium)

1986
Won first AFC Championship, beating the Miami Dolphins

31 FINAL SCORE **14**

2000
Drafted quarterback Tom Brady

2002

Won Super Bowl 36, beating the St. Louis Rams

20   FINAL SCORE   **17**

2004

Won Super Bowl 38, beating the Carolina Panthers

32   FINAL SCORE   **29**

2015

Won Super Bowl 49, beating the Seattle Seahawks

28   FINAL SCORE   **24**

2005

Won Super Bowl 39, beating the Philadelphia Eagles

24   FINAL SCORE   **21**

2007

Had a 16-0 record in the regular season

In the 1960s, Gino Cappelletti became the first Patriots star. He was a **kicker** and wide receiver. **Guard** John Hannah was the first Patriot to get into the Pro Football Hall of Fame.

John Hannah

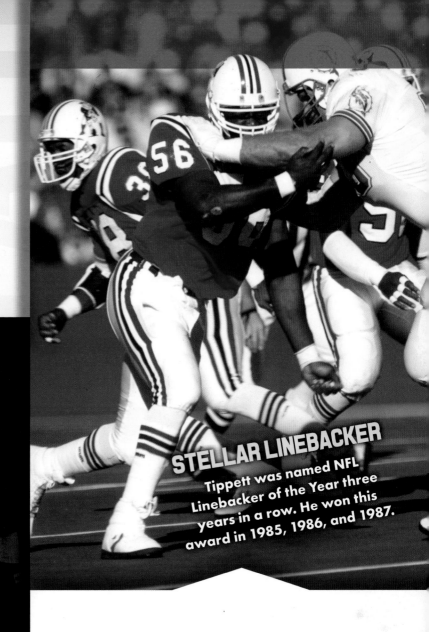

STELLAR LINEBACKER

Tippett was named NFL Linebacker of the Year three years in a row. He won this award in 1985, 1986, and 1987.

Andre Tippett and Tedy Bruschi were star **linebackers**. They supported the Patriots' **defense**.

Tom Brady proved to be a calm leader when he took the field. In 2007, he became the first quarterback to throw 50 touchdown passes in one season.

Brady and Coach Belichick have earned multiple Most Valuable Player and Coach of the Year awards. In 2007 and 2010, they received these awards at the same time.

TEAM GREATS

GINO CAPPELLETTI
WIDE RECEIVER AND
KICKER
1960-1970

JOHN HANNAH
GUARD
1973-1985

ANDRE TIPPETT
LINEBACKER
1982-1993

Tom Brady

LOW DRAFT PICK
Tom Brady was drafted in the 6th round. He was the 199th overall selection out of 254 draft picks.

TEDY BRUSCHI
LINEBACKER
1996-2008

BILL BELICHICK
HEAD COACH
2000-PRESENT

TOM BRADY
QUARTERBACK
2000-PRESENT

The Patriots' old logo was an American patriot snapping a football. He wore a **minuteman** uniform. Fan traditions still use this idea.

A group called the End Zone Militia helps fans celebrate. They wear minutemen uniforms. They fire **muskets** when the Patriots score.

End Zone Militia

Patriots fans are wild and loyal. They sit in cold snowstorms to cheer on their team. Fans from all over New England cover themselves in red, white, and blue.

They are proud of their minutemen hats. These fans expect more Super Bowl wins. The Patriots' dynasty gives fans much to celebrate!

MORE ABOUT THE
PATRIOTS

Team name:
New England Patriots

Team name explained:
Named after American patriots who fought against the British in the Revolutionary War

Joined NFL: 1970
(AFL from 1960-1969)

Conference: **AFC**

Division: **East**

Main rivals:
New York Jets, Buffalo Bills

Hometown:
Foxborough, Massachusetts

Training camp location:
Gillette Stadium Practice Fields,
Foxborough, Massachusetts

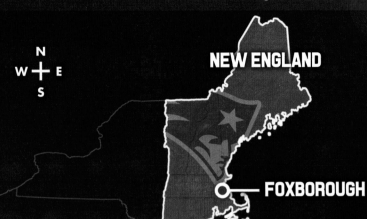

NEW ENGLAND

N
W — E
S

FOXBOROUGH

Home stadium name: Gillette Stadium

Stadium opened: 2002

Seats in stadium: 66,829

Logo: A silver patriot
called the "Flying Elvis,"
with a navy blue and
red striped hat

Colors: Red, white,
blue, silver

Mascot: Pat Patriot

GLOSSARY

conference—a large grouping of sports teams that often play one another

cornerback—a player on defense whose main job is to stop wide receivers from catching passes

defense—the group of players who try to stop the opposing team from scoring

division—a small grouping of sports teams that often play one another; usually there are several divisions of teams in a conference.

drafted—chose a college athlete to play for a professional team

dynasty—a team that succeeds for many years

guard—a player on offense whose job is to tackle opposing linemen

interception—a catch made by a defensive player of a pass thrown by the opposing team

kicker—a player whose main job is to kick extra points, field goals, and kickoffs

linebackers—players on defense whose main jobs are to make tackles and stop catches; linebackers stand just behind the defensive linemen.

minuteman—a volunteer soldier in the American Revolutionary War who was ready to fight at a minute's notice

muskets—long guns used by soldiers before rifles were invented

New England—an area in the northeastern United States that includes Connecticut, Maine, Massachusetts, New Hampshire, Rhode Island, and Vermont

quarterback—a player on offense whose main job is to throw and hand off the ball

rival—a long-standing opponent

Super Bowl—the championship game for the NFL

wide receiver—a player on offense whose main job is to catch passes from the quarterback

TO LEARN MORE

AT THE LIBRARY

Whiting, Jim. *The Story of the New England Patriots.* Mankato, Minn.: Creative Paperbacks, 2014.

Wyner, Zach. *New England Patriots.* New York, N.Y.: AV2 by Weigl, 2015.

Zappa, Marcia. *New England Patriots.* Edina, Minn.: ABDO Pub. Company, 2015.

ON THE WEB

Learning more about the New England Patriots is as easy as 1, 2, 3.

1. Go to www.factsurfer.com.

2. Enter "New England Patriots" into the search box.

3. Click the "Surf" button and you will see a list of related web sites.

With factsurfer.com, finding more information is just a click away.

INDEX